United States Government Accountability Office

Report to Congressional Requesters

I0415797

February 2012

BUREAU OF PRISONS

Eligibility and Capacity Impact Use of Flexibilities to Reduce Inmates' Time in Prison

GAO
Accountability ★ Integrity ★ Reliability

GAO-12-320

G A O
Accountability * Integrity * Reliability

Highlights

Highlights of GAO-12-320, a report to congressional requesters

BUREAU OF PRISONS

Eligibility and Capacity Impact Use of Flexibilities to Reduce Inmates' Time in Prison

Why GAO Did This Study

The Department of Justice's Federal Bureau of Prisons (BOP) is responsible for the custody and care of federal offenders. BOP's population has increased from about 145,000 in 2000 to about 217,000 in 2011 and BOP is operating at 38 percent over capacity. There is no longer parole for federal offenders and BOP has limited authority to affect the length of an inmate's prison sentence. BOP has some statutory authorities and programs to reduce the amount of time an inmate remains in prison, which when balanced with BOP's mission to protect public safety and prepare inmates for reentry, can help reduce crowding and the costs of incarceration. GAO was asked to address: (1) the extent to which BOP utilizes its authorities to reduce a federal prisoner's period of incarceration; and (2) what factors, if any, impact BOP's use of these authorities. GAO analyzed relevant laws and BOP policies; obtained nationwide data on inmate participation in relevant programs and sentence reductions from fiscal years 2009 through 2011; conducted site visits to nine BOP institutions selected to cover a range of prison characteristics and at each, interviewed officials responsible for relevant programs; and visited four community-based facilities serving the institutions visited. Though not generalizable, the information obtained from these visits provided insights.

What GAO Recommends

GAO recommends that BOP establish a plan, including time frames and milestones, for requiring contractors to submit prices of RRC beds and home detention services. BOP concurred with this recommendation.

View GAO-12-320. For more information, contact David C. Maurer at (202) 512-9627 or maurerd@gao.gov.

What GAO Found

BOP's use of authorities to reduce a federal prisoner's period of incarceration varies. BOP primarily utilizes three authorities—the Residential Drug Abuse Treatment Program (RDAP), community corrections, and good conduct time.

- Eligible inmates can participate in RDAP before release from prison, but those eligible for a sentence reduction are generally unable to complete RDAP in time to earn the maximum reduction (generally 12 months). During fiscal years 2009 through 2011, of the 15,302 inmates who completed RDAP and were eligible for a sentence reduction, 2,846 (19 percent) received the maximum reduction and the average reduction was 8.0 months. BOP officials said that participants generally do not receive the maximum reduction because they have less than 12 months to serve when they complete RDAP.

- To facilitate inmates' reintegration into society, BOP may transfer eligible inmates to community corrections locations for up to the final 12 months of their sentences. Inmates may spend this time in contract residential re-entry centers (RRCs)—also known as halfway houses—and in detention in their homes for up to 6 months. Based on the most recently available data, almost 29,000 inmates completed their sentences through community corrections in fiscal year 2010, after an average placement of about 4 months; 17,672 in RRCs, 11,094 in RRCs then home detention, and 145 in home detention only. RRCs monitor inmates in home detention and charge BOP 50 percent of the daily RRC cost to do so. However, BOP does not require RRC contractors to separate the price of home detention services from the price of RRC beds and thus, does not know the actual costs of home detention. BOP officials stated that they are developing a process to review and amend existing RRC contracts and require new contractors to submit proposals separating out RRC and home detention prices, but did not document the specifics of the review process or establish time frames or milestones for the review. Thus, BOP does not have a roadmap for how it will achieve this goal.

- Most eligible inmates receive all of their potential good conduct time credit for exemplary compliance with institutional disciplinary regulations—54 days taken off their sentence, per year served, if an inmate has earned or is earning a high school diploma; 42 days if not. As of the end of fiscal years 2009, 2010, and 2011, about 87 percent of inmates had earned all of their available credit.

BOP also has other authorities, such as releasing prisoners early for very specialized reasons, but has used these less frequently for various reasons.

Inmate eligibility and lack of capacity impact BOP's use of certain flexibilities and programs that can reduce an inmate's time in prison. BOP officials cited inmate ineligibility for RRC placement (e.g., inmates who are likely to escape or be arrested or with sentences of 6 months or less, among other things) as the primary reason that some inmates are not released through community corrections and one of the main reasons that some inmates are not able to participate in RDAP. BOP's lack of additional RRC space has prevented it from increasing the length of its RRC placements. According to BOP, lack of program capacity also prevents eligible inmates from entering and completing RDAP early enough to earn their maximum allowable sentence reductions, which prevents BOP from maximizing the cost savings provided by the authority.

_____ **United States Government Accountability Office**

Contents

Letter		1
	Background	5
	BOP's Use of Authorities That Can Reduce a Federal Prisoner's Period of Incarceration Varies	10
	Inmate Eligibility and Lack of Capacity Impact BOP's Use of Certain Flexibilities	30
	Conclusions	35
	Recommendation for Executive Action	36
	Agency Comments and Our Evaluation	36

Appendix I	Comments from the Federal Bureau of Prisons	38

Appendix II	GAO Contact and Staff Acknowledgments	39

Tables

	Table 1: Statutory Provisions Available to BOP to Reduce a Federal Prisoner's Period of Incarceration or Time in BOP Custody	8
	Table 2: Number of Eligible Inmates Placed in Community Corrections Who Complete Their Sentences, and Average Length of Stay for Fiscal Years 2009 and 2010	17
	Table 3: GCT Credit Disallowance Guidelines, by Infraction Severity Level	22
	Table 4: Illustration of BOP's Calculation of GCT Credit for an Imposed Sentence of 10 years for an Inmate Earning the Maximum GCT Credit	24

Figures

	Figure 1: BOP Regional Map	6
	Figure 2: RDAP Participation Process	12
	Figure 3: Daily Cost per Inmate of BOP Facilities Compared with Community Corrections	19
	Figure 4: Number of Inmates Ineligible for RRC Placement from April 2008 to March 2011	31

United States Government Accountability Office
Washington, DC 20548

February 7, 2012

The Honorable Patrick J. Leahy
Chairman
Committee on the Judiciary
United States Senate

The Honorable Robert C. "Bobby" Scott
Ranking Member
Subcommittee on Crime, Terrorism, and Homeland Security
Committee on the Judiciary
United States House of Representatives

The Department of Justice's (DOJ) Federal Bureau of Prisons (BOP) is responsible for the custody and care of federal offenders.[1] BOP's mission is to confine federal offenders in the controlled, safe, secure, humane, and cost-efficient environments of prisons and community-based facilities, and to provide work and other self-improvement opportunities to assist offenders in becoming law-abiding citizens. BOP's population has increased by 50 percent from about 145,000 in 2000 to about 217,000 at the close of fiscal year 2011, and BOP projects a net increase of roughly 6,000 inmates annually for the next 3 years. In addition, BOP reports that it is operating at 38 percent over capacity with higher rates of crowding in its high- and medium-security institutions than in its low- and minimum-security institutions.[2]

The size of the federal prison population is a function of many factors, including the nation's crime levels, sentencing laws, and law enforcement policies, all of which are beyond the control of BOP. In addition, the Sentencing Reform Act of 1984 abolished parole for federal offenders,

---

[1] The National Capital Revitalization and Self-Government Improvement Act of 1997, Pub. L. No. 105-33, § 11201, 111 Stat. 712, 734-37, transferred the responsibility and costs associated with certain state criminal justice functions, including housing, parole, and supervised release of adult felons convicted under the D.C. Code from the District of Columbia to various federal government agencies, including BOP.

[2] The figure refers to capacity in institutions operated by BOP. Security level classification depends on factors such as staff supervision the institution is able to provide; the presence of security towers; perimeter barriers; the type of inmate housing (e.g., dormitories, cubicles, or cells); and the staff-to-inmate ratio.

GAO-12-320 BOP Use of Sentencing Flexibilities

and subsequent legislation established mandatory minimum sentences for many federal offenses, which limit the authority BOP has to affect the size of the prison population or the length of prison sentences.[3] However, BOP has some statutory authorities whereby it can reduce the period during which an inmate is incarcerated or remains in BOP custody.[4] These programs and authorities are primarily intended to rehabilitate inmates and prepare them for reentry into society, and encourage good behavior while in BOP custody. Effective BOP use of these authorities, while adhering to the agency's stated mission to protect society by confining offenders in the controlled environments of prisons and community-based facilities, has the potential to help reduce overcrowding and the associated costs of incarceration.

You asked us to review the authorities BOP has to reduce a federal prisoner's period of incarceration and how it is using its authorities. Specifically, this report addresses the following questions:

- To what extent does BOP utilize its authorities to reduce a federal prisoner's period of incarceration?
- What factors, if any, impact BOP's use of these authorities?

To address the first question, we analyzed relevant federal statutes to identify what discretionary authorities BOP has to reduce a prisoner's period of incarceration.[5] We also analyzed BOP policies, program statements, and guidance memos, and interviewed officials from BOP's

---

[3] Prior to passage of the Sentencing Reform Act of 1984, Pub. L. No. 98-473, 98 Stat. 1987, federal judges generally had broad discretion in sentencing. Most criminal statutes provided only broad maximum terms of imprisonment. Federal law outlined the maximum sentence, federal judges imposed a sentence within a statutory range, and the federal parole official eventually determined the actual duration of incarceration.

[4] In this report, we use the term "incarceration" to refer to inmates housed in federal correctional institutions or privately managed prisons. Most inmates serve out the last portion of their sentences under BOP custody in a prerelease placement in a community-based facility or in home detention.

[5] We limited our review to authorities that apply to inmates who committed a federal offense on or after November 1, 1987, after the effective date of the Sentencing Reform Act of 1984, also known as "new law." BOP also has in its custody offenders sentenced under "old law," some of whom are parole eligible, and may not be eligible to benefit from some of the authorities we discuss in this report. "Old law" refers to offenses committed before November 1, 1987, and to the statutory, regulatory, and BOP provisions followed prior to the enactment of the Comprehensive Crime Control Act of 1984, Pub. L. No. 98-473, 98 Stat. 1976.

Information, Policy, & Public Affairs Division; Office of General Counsel; Designation and Sentence Computation Center; and Correctional Programs Division to determine how BOP implements programs that utilize its discretionary authorities. We obtained nationwide data regarding inmate participation in relevant BOP programs, program capacity, and sentence reductions received for program participation, or through other authorities, during fiscal years 2009, 2010, and 2011. We also obtained population and cost projections BOP has developed related to various alternative uses of its authorities. We compared BOP's methods for estimating the costs of supervising inmates in home detention with standard practices for program and project management to determine whether BOP has a planning process in place to achieve reliable estimates of these costs.[6] We obtained information from relevant BOP officials about the steps taken to ensure the accuracy of all of the data, and found the data to be sufficiently reliable for the purposes of this report.

To address the second question, we interviewed BOP Central Office and program officials as well as subject matter experts in community corrections, inmate rights, and in-prison rehabilitation programs identified through a review of the literature and through subsequent discussions with these experts. We also conducted site visits to six BOP institutions, and one privately managed institution overseen by BOP, to observe operations and to obtain perspectives from prison officials about the implementation of these discretionary authorities and any challenges they faced. We selected facilities to cover a range of prison characteristics, including management (e.g., BOP and private), security classification (e.g., minimum, low, medium, and high), medical care level, inmate gender, geographic variability (e.g., region, urban/rural), and the presence of relevant BOP programs.[7] The sites include four BOP institutions and one privately managed institution in BOP's Western Region (all in California); and four institutions in BOP's Mid-Atlantic Region (all in

---

[6] The Project Management Institute, *The Standard for Program Management* © (2006).

[7] According to BOP officials, care-level categories are based on both medical treatment capacity and proximity to an outside hospital. Care-level 1 facilities can treat limited medical needs, and are generally about 40-60 miles from a hospital; care-level 2 facilities can treat stable diseases, and are generally about 20-30 miles from a hospital; care-level 3 facilities can provide nursing care and assisted living, as well as mental health treatment, and are generally about 5-10 miles from a hospital; care-level 4 facilities are generally hospitals, of which there are six in BOP's system.

Maryland, Virginia, and West Virginia). Five of the nine institutions contained multiple facilities which housed offenders classified at different security levels.[8] At each institution, we obtained perspectives on challenges from those officials responsible for the following activities:

- conducting disciplinary hearings which could result in the disallowance of sentence-reduction credit received by inmates for good conduct while incarcerated;
- administering BOP's substance abuse treatment programs, including the Residential Drug Abuse Treatment Program (RDAP) which provides sentence reductions for eligible inmates who successfully complete the program; and
- reviewing inmates' cases to make recommendations regarding the length of placement in residential re-entry centers (RRCs), also known as halfway houses, or in home detention at the end of an individual's sentence.

We also visited four RRCs in the Los Angeles and Washington, D.C. metropolitan areas—the closest major metropolitan areas to the prisons we visited, and thus serving inmates released to community corrections from these prisons—to discuss with BOP community corrections officials overseeing the operation of these RRCs and RRC managers any factors that facilitate or hinder placing inmates in the community. We cannot generalize our work from the facilities and offices we visited to BOP facilities nationwide, but the information we obtained provides insights into how BOP implements its discretionary authorities in various locations.

We conducted this performance audit from June 2011 to February 2012 in accordance with generally accepted government auditing standards. Those standards require that we plan and perform the audit to obtain sufficient, appropriate evidence to provide a reasonable basis for our findings and conclusions based on our audit objectives. We believe that

---

[8] The nine institutions we visited contained the following 15 facilities housing offenders at different security levels: 1 high-security facility, 3 medium-security facilities, 4 low-security facilities, 5 minimum-security facilities, 1 facility housing female offenders of various security levels, and 1 administrative facility housing both male and female inmates. BOP designates certain institutions with special missions as "administrative," such as the detention of pretrial offenders; the treatment of inmates with serious or chronic medical problems; or the containment of extremely dangerous, violent, or escape-prone inmates. These institutions may house offenders at several different security levels.

GAO-12-320 BOP Use of Sentencing Flexibilities

the evidence obtained provides a reasonable basis for our findings and conclusions based on our audit objectives.

Background

BOP Population and Institutions

In fiscal year 2012, BOP had a budget of about $6.6 billion for salaries and expenses and as of December 2011, BOP had a staff of about 38,000, which includes administrative, program, and support staff responsible for all of BOP's activities nationwide. BOP houses inmates across six geographic regions in 117 federal institutions, 15 privately managed prisons, 185 RRCs (also known as halfway houses), and home detention.[9] At the close of fiscal year 2011, about 94 percent of BOP's inmate population was incarcerated in either federal institutions or privately managed prisons, operating at four different security level designations: minimum, low, medium, and high. The designations depend on the level of security and staff supervision the institution is able to provide such as the presence of security towers; perimeter barriers; the type of inmate housing, including dormitory, cubicle, or cell-type housing; and the staff-to-inmate ratio. Some BOP institutions include multiple prison facilities with different security classifications under common management, in part to increase cost efficiencies.[10] According to BOP, privately managed low-security facilities primarily house criminal aliens.[11] Figure 1 shows the distribution of BOP institutions, privately managed prisons, and RRCs across BOP's six geographic regions.

---

[9] BOP contracts with four private corrections companies. BOP's privately managed prisons operate under performance-based contracts in accordance with some BOP policies. BOP also has agreements with state and local governments and contracts with privately operated facilities for the detention of federally adjudicated juveniles and for the secure detention of some short-term federal inmates.

[10] BOP has 13 federal correctional complexes systemwide that include separate prisons under common management, and many prisons include an adjacent minimum-security satellite camp under common management.

[11] Criminal aliens are noncitizens convicted of crimes while in this country legally or illegally.

Figure 1: BOP Regional Map, Fiscal Year 2011

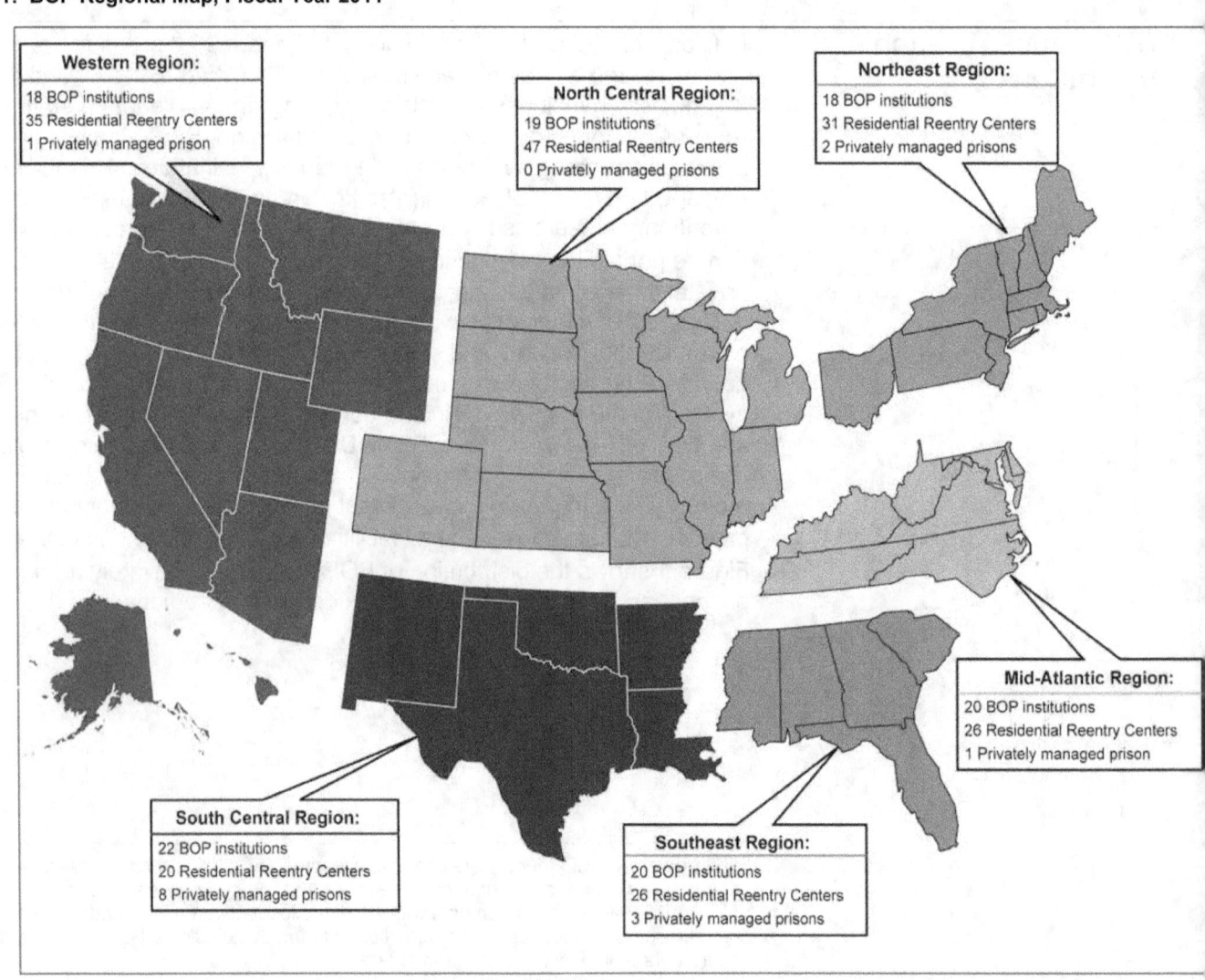

Source: GAO analysis of BOP data.

To house inmates in community corrections locations, BOP contracts with private organizations to manage 185 RRCs around the country.[12] These RRCs allow BOP to house inmates outside of a prison environment to either serve out their full sentence or their remaining sentence prior to release in the community.[13] Inmates are authorized to leave for approved activities, such as seeking employment, working, counseling, visiting, or recreation, but are monitored 24 hours a day through sign-out procedures, regular head counts, staff visits to the approved locations, and random phone contacts. Inmates in RRCs are also required to work, or be actively seeking work, and to pay a percentage of their salaries as a subsistence fee to cover some of their expenses at the RRC. Some federal inmates are placed on home detention at the end of their prison term, either directly from an institution, or following some time in an RRC. Home detention describes all circumstances under which an inmate is serving a portion of his or her sentence while residing in his or her home. Home detention inmates are held to strict schedules and curfews and are monitored by a nearby RRC or the U.S. Probation Office through random staff visits, phone contacts, and occasionally through the use of electronic monitoring.[14] At the close of fiscal year 2011, about 5 percent of the inmate population was housed in RRCs or home detention.

BOP Discretionary Authorities That Can Reduce a Prisoner's Period of Incarceration or Time in BOP Custody

BOP has a number of discretionary authorities it can use to impact the period during which an inmate is incarcerated or remains in BOP custody. According to BOP officials, many of the programs that arise from these authorities are primarily intended to rehabilitate inmates and prepare them for reentry into society, as well as encourage good behavior while in BOP custody. The authorities can be classified into two main categories: (1) authorities that reduce the length of the inmate's sentence, and (2)

---

[12] As of December 1, 2011, BOP contracted with 105 providers to manage its inmates in RRCs and home detention.

[13] According to BOP officials, inmates serve out their full sentences in an RRC only if recommended by the sentencing judge, if the inmate does not pose a threat to public safety, and as bed space in RRCs allow. From fiscal years 2009 through 2011, 30 inmates served out their full sentences in an RRC.

[14] BOP's community-based programs are administered by staff of the Correctional Programs Division (CPD) in Central Office (in Washington, D.C.), community corrections regional management teams in each of BOP's 6 regional offices, and the employees of 22 community corrections management (CCM) field offices serving specific judicial districts within their regions.

authorities that allow BOP to transfer an inmate out of prison to serve the remainder of his or her sentence in an RRC or home detention. Table 1 provides the statutory provisions allowing for BOP discretion to reduce a federal prisoner's period of incarceration.[15]

Table 1: Statutory Provisions Available to BOP to Reduce a Federal Prisoner's Period of Incarceration or Time in BOP Custody

Discretionary flexibilities and associated statutory provisions	Description
Sentence credits and sentence reduction	
Good Conduct Time (GCT) 18 U.S.C. § 3624(b)	BOP is authorized to award credit toward the service of an inmate's sentence, beyond the time served, of up to 54 days per year of sentence served if the inmate has displayed exemplary compliance with institutional disciplinary regulations. To be eligible to earn credit, the inmate must be serving a sentence of more than 1 year other than a term of imprisonment for life.
Residential Drug Abuse Treatment Program (RDAP) 18 U.S.C. § 3621(e)	BOP is required to provide substance abuse treatment for each inmate it determines has a treatable condition of substance abuse. BOP must, subject to the availability of appropriations, provide residential substance abuse treatment (and make arrangements for appropriate aftercare) for all eligible inmates, with priority for the treatment provided based on proximity to release date. BOP may reduce the sentence of an inmate convicted of a nonviolent offense who successfully completes residential substance abuse treatment for a period of up to 1 year.

[15] Under 18 U.S.C. § 4102, the Attorney General is authorized to transfer offenders under a sentence of imprisonment, on parole, or on probation to the foreign countries of which they are citizens or nationals, and to delegate such authority to officers in DOJ. The United States currently has treaties with 76 countries to return American citizens incarcerated in those countries to the United States to serve out their sentences, and to transfer foreign national inmates serving sentences in the United States to serve out their terms in the countries where they are citizens or nationals. Within DOJ, BOP shares responsibility with the Criminal Division, the United States Attorneys' Offices, and the United States Marshals Service for administering the treaty transfer program. BOP is responsible for explaining the program to foreign national inmates, determining if a current treaty agreement exists for interested inmates and if those inmates are eligible for transfer, and preparing application packets for eligible inmates which are reviewed by the Criminal Division's International Prisoner Transfer Unit. Because DOJ's Office of Inspector General (OIG) conducted a separate review of this program during the course of our work, we do not discuss this program in our report. See: Department of Justice, Office of Inspector General, *The Department of Justice's International Prisoner Transfer Program* (Washington, D.C.: December 2011).

Discretionary flexibilities and associated statutory provisions	Description
Modification of an Imposed Sentence 18 U.S.C. § 3582(c)	Upon motion of the Director of BOP, the court may reduce a term of imprisonment after considering certain factors if it finds that either (1) extraordinary and compelling reasons warrant such a reduction; or (2) the inmate is at least 70 years of age, has served at least 30 years in prison for the offense or offenses for which the inmate is imprisoned, and a determination has been made by the Director of BOP that the inmate is not a danger to the safety of any other person or the community; and that such a reduction is consistent with applicable policy statements issued by the U.S. Sentencing Commission (USSC).[a] The Director may also motion the court for an inmate who has been sentenced to a term of imprisonment based on a sentencing range that has subsequently been lowered by the USSC and the court may reduce the term of imprisonment.
Weekend and Holiday Release 18 U.S.C. § 3624a	BOP is authorized to release inmates whose release date falls on Saturday, Sunday, or a legal holiday on the last preceding weekday.
Sentence Computation Authority to Allow Concurrent Service of Federal and State Sentences 18 U.S.C. § 3584 (Multiple sentences of imprisonment)	If multiple sentences are imposed as the result of a single trial from a single indictment, generally the terms run concurrently (with a concurrent sentence, two or more sentences of imprisonment are to be served simultaneously) unless the federal court or a statute requires the terms to be served consecutively. However, if multiple sentences are imposed as a result of different trials, as when federal and state sentences are imposed on a defendant, generally the terms run consecutively (with consecutive sentences, two or more sentences of imprisonment are to be served in sequence) unless the federal court or a statute requires the terms to be served concurrently. When both a federal and a state court have imposed prison sentences on an offender, BOP may credit time served in a state institution towards an inmate's federal sentence in certain circumstances.
Credit for Time Served in Custody 18 U.S.C. § 3585(b)	An inmate must be given credit toward his or her prison term for any time spent in official detention prior to the date the sentence commences as a result of the offense for which the sentence was imposed, or as a result of any other charge for which the inmate was arrested after commission of the offense for which the sentence was imposed.
Transfer from prison to community setting	
Residential Reentry and Home Detention 18 U.S.C. § 3624(c)	The Director of BOP must, to the extent practicable, ensure that an inmate spends a portion of the final months of that inmate's term (not to exceed 12 months), under conditions that will afford the inmate a reasonable opportunity to adjust to and prepare for reentry into the community. This may include a prisoner being placed in an RRC. In addition, a prisoner may be placed in home detention for the shorter of 10 percent of the term of imprisonment or 6 months.

Discretionary flexibilities and associated statutory provisions	Description
Elderly Offender Pilot Program 42 U.S.C. § 17541(g)	The Attorney General was required to conduct a pilot program during fiscal years 2009 and 2010 to determine the effectiveness of removing eligible elderly offenders from a BOP facility and placing such offenders on home detention until the expiration of the prison term to which the offender was sentenced.
Both sentence credit and transfer to community setting	
Shock Incarceration Program 18 U.S.C. § 4046	BOP may place in a shock incarceration program (also known as a boot camp) any person who is sentenced to a term of imprisonment of more than 12, but not more than 30, months, if such person consents to that placement. BOP discontinued all shock incarceration programs in 2005, though it continues to retain the statutory authority to institute such programs.

Source: GAO analysis of federal statutes.

[a] Created in 1984, the United States Sentencing Commission (USSC) was charged with developing the federal sentencing guidelines to limit disparities in sentencing among offenders with similar criminal backgrounds found guilty of similar crimes.

BOP's Use of Authorities That Can Reduce a Federal Prisoner's Period of Incarceration Varies

Eligible Prisoners Can Participate in RDAP in Time to Complete the Program; Few Receive the Maximum Sentence Reduction

BOP is required, subject to the availability of appropriations, to provide residential substance abuse treatment and make arrangements for appropriate aftercare for all eligible prisoners.[16] Generally, the process to determine inmate eligibility for RDAP participation begins when inmates express interest in the program.[17] In June 1995, BOP began offering nonviolent participants a sentence reduction incentive of up to 12 months

---

[16] 18 U.S.C. § 3621(e). During the 500-hour institution component of RDAP, participants are separated from the inmate general population in order to support prosocial attitudes and behaviors and isolate program participants from negative peer pressure in the larger prison environment.

[17] Court documents, such as the Presentence Investigation Report, often include substance use information, but other documentation may be sufficient, such as from a medical provider, probation officer, or social service professional.

for successful completion of the program.[18] The amount of sentence reduction awarded upon completion is based on the length of an inmate's sentence.[19] Figure 2 displays the process by which inmates enter and complete RDAP, and receive a sentence reduction if eligible.

---

[18] Violent Crime Control and Law Enforcement Act of 1994, Pub. L. No. 103-322, § 32001, 108 Stat. 1796, 1896-98. RDAP was originally developed in 1989 and the first participants completed the program in fiscal year 1990. Once requested, BOP is to determine an inmate's early release eligibility status based on a review of the inmate's current offense and prior convictions. BOP reviews current and prior offenses for both U.S. Code and D.C. Code felony offenders. According to BOP headquarters officials, the legal review is ordinarily completed within 30 days, but may take longer for more complicated cases.

[19] BOP implemented the RDAP maximum sentence reduction categories based on an inmate's sentence length in fiscal year 2009 as a policy decision, but the first inmates to receive sentence reductions based on the new policy completed the program in fiscal year 2010; the authorizing statute gives BOP discretion over how to provide up to a 12-month sentence reduction to eligible RDAP participants.

Figure 2: RDAP Participation Process

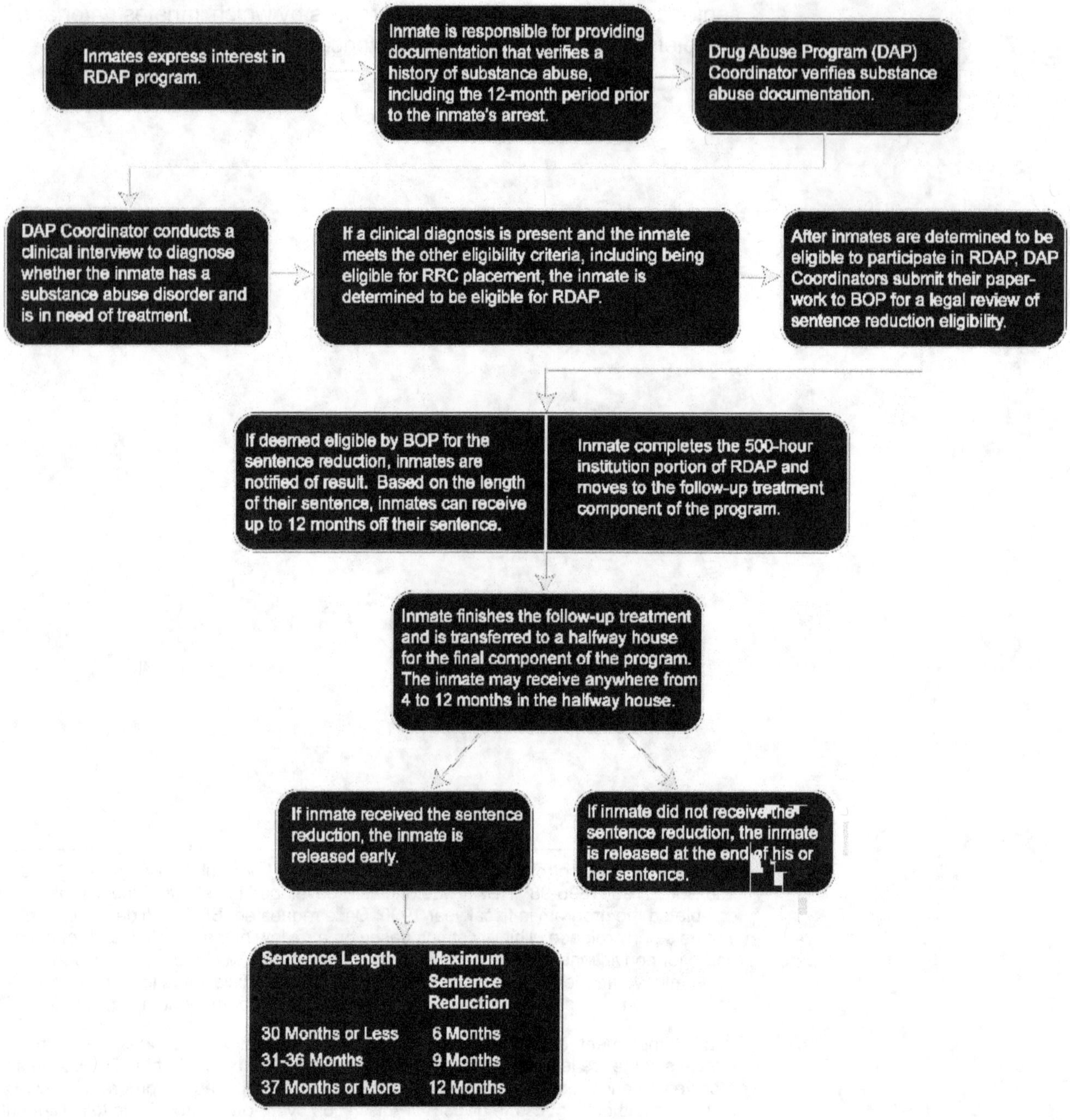

Inmates express interest in RDAP program.

Inmate is responsible for providing documentation that verifies a history of substance abuse, including the 12-month period prior to the inmate's arrest.

Drug Abuse Program (DAP) Coordinator verifies substance abuse documentation.

DAP Coordinator conducts a clinical interview to diagnose whether the inmate has a substance abuse disorder and is in need of treatment.

If a clinical diagnosis is present and the inmate meets the other eligibility criteria, including being eligible for RRC placement, the inmate is determined to be eligible for RDAP.

After inmates are determined to be eligible to participate in RDAP, DAP Coordinators submit their paperwork to BOP for a legal review of sentence reduction eligibility.

If deemed eligible by BOP for the sentence reduction, inmates are notified of result. Based on the length of their sentence, inmates can receive up to 12 months off their sentence.

Inmate completes the 500-hour institution portion of RDAP and moves to the follow-up treatment component of the program.

Inmate finishes the follow-up treatment and is transferred to a halfway house for the final component of the program. The inmate may receive anywhere from 4 to 12 months in the halfway house.

If inmate received the sentence reduction, the inmate is released early.

If inmate did not receive the sentence reduction, the inmate is released at the end of his or her sentence.

Sentence Length	Maximum Sentence Reduction
30 Months or Less	6 Months
31-36 Months	9 Months
37 Months or More	12 Months

Source: GAO analysis of BOP data and documentation.

According to BOP's annual reports to Congress on substance abuse treatment programs, during fiscal years 2009 and 2010 all eligible inmates who expressed interest in RDAP were able to participate in the program in time to complete it before their release from BOP custody. BOP officials stated that all eligible inmates were again able to participate in RDAP in fiscal year 2011. BOP estimates that 40 percent of inmates entering federal custody each year will have a substance abuse disorder and thus may be eligible to participate in RDAP, provided the other eligibility criteria are met.[20] BOP data show that from fiscal years 2009 through 2011, on average, 18,709 inmates participated in RDAP in the 62 program locations throughout BOP each year. However, BOP reports RDAP participation numbers as an aggregate count of every inmate who participated in the program at some point during a given fiscal year. This includes inmates who failed to complete the program—for example in fiscal year 2011, according to BOP, 17 percent of inmates left the program due to expulsion, withdrawal, disciplinary transfers, or other reasons—and inmates who entered the program in a prior fiscal year or who will complete the program in a subsequent fiscal year. As a result, inmates may be double-counted—reported as participants in multiple fiscal years. The participation numbers reported annually to Congress thus do not reflect how many individual inmates participate in or successfully complete RDAP each fiscal year. However, BOP provided us with data showing that from fiscal years 2009 through 2011, on average, 6,875 inmates completed RDAP each year.

While BOP has reported that all eligible and interested inmates are able to complete RDAP before their release from BOP custody, those eligible for a sentence reduction incentive for successful completion are generally unable to complete the program in time to benefit from the maximum allowable reduction. From fiscal years 2009 through 2011, 15,302 RDAP participants completed the program and were eligible to receive a sentence reduction. Of those 15,302 participants eligible for a sentence reduction, 14,034 were eligible for a maximum sentence reduction of 12 months, 596 were eligible for 9 months, and 672 were eligible for 6 months. However, in these three fiscal years, 2,846 inmates (19 percent) received the maximum sentence reduction that corresponded to their sentence length, while 190 (1 percent) received no sentence reduction.

---

[20] BOP's projection is based on a study of inmates entering federal custody from fiscal years 2002 through 2003.

The average sentence reduction received by eligible participants was 8.0 months.[21]

Eligible participants generally do not receive the maximum allowable sentence reduction because, according to BOP officials, by the time they complete RDAP, they have fewer months remaining on their sentences than the maximum allowable reduction. For example, to allow enough time for completion of RDAP in the institution (9 to 12 months) and transitional drug abuse treatment in an RRC, BOP policy recommends that Drug Abuse Program (DAP) Coordinators initiate the eligibility screening process no less than 24 months prior to the inmate's projected release date. However, some inmates may have to wait for clinical interviews, for program slots to open, or both.[22] For example, at one institution we visited, BOP officials told us they had a queue of 50 inmates waiting to be interviewed by the DAP Coordinator to determine program eligibility. At another institution we visited, BOP officials told us they had a queue of 66 inmates who had been approved for participation and were waiting for program slots to open. According to BOP, delays resulting from this systemwide demand can prevent timely inmate entry into RDAP and can reduce the number of eligible inmates receiving the maximum allowable sentence reduction.[23]

---

[21] The maximum average sentence reduction would be 11.6 months, since 1,268 of the 15,302 inmates who completed the program in fiscal years 2009 through 2011 were eligible for a maximum reduction of 6 or 9 months, based on the length of their sentences.

[22] The RDAP program is available in 62 locations. BOP officials stated that potential needs for substance abuse treatment are considered by BOP in initial designation to a BOP institution following sentencing. Also, eligible inmates residing in facilities without RDAP may have to wait to transfer to a facility offering the program.

[23] According to BOP officials, inmates enter RDAP as cohorts, with 24 inmates per staff member, and programs may have several cohorts participating concurrently. Inmates on the waiting list wait until the next available cohort begins.

BOP Refers Eligible Prisoners to Community Corrections, but Has Not Assessed Home Detention to Determine Potential Cost Savings

As a part of an inmate's reintegration into the community, BOP attempts to provide all eligible inmates the opportunity to participate in community corrections, defined as RRCs and home detention services.[24] BOP's program statements for RRCs and home detention lay out the steps all BOP institutions are required to follow to assess each inmate for community corrections suitability and appropriate length of placement. During an assessment for RRC placement, BOP policy requires prerelease RRC placement decisions be made on an individual basis and conducted in a manner consistent with certain statutory criteria. The criteria are: (1) the resources of the facility contemplated, (2) the nature and circumstances of the offense, (3) the history and characteristics of the prisoner, (4) any statement by the court that imposed the sentence, and (5) any pertinent policy statement issued by the USSC.[25] According to BOP officials, these factors are applied to all inmates regardless of security level or offense. However, to place inmates on home detention, BOP uses these factors as well as other factors stated in its home detention program statement. The Program Statement requires community corrections personnel to consider whether:

- BOP has applied a public safety factor, indicating that the inmate has demonstrated certain behaviors that require increased security measures to ensure the protection of society;
- BOP has designated the inmate as a Central Inmate Monitoring case, indicating that the inmate requires a higher level of review prior to any movement outside the institution;
- the inmate's case is sensitive or high profile and might generate undue public concern;
- the inmate has a history of escape or prior community corrections failure; or
- the inmate is unlikely to be employed.

---

[24] The Second Chance Act of 2007, Pub. L. No. 110-199, § 251(a), 122 Stat. 657, 692-93, amended 18 U.S.C. § 3624(c) to enable BOP to place inmates in community corrections for up to 12 months (previously limited to 6 months or 10 percent of an inmate's sentence), and home detention for the shorter of 10 percent of the term of imprisonment or 6 months. The statute does not guarantee an inmate a 1-year RRC placement or placement in home detention for any portion of the inmate's sentence, but only directs BOP to consider placing an inmate in a RRC for up to the final 12 months of the sentence, and to consider using home detention as part of an inmate's reiintegration into the community.

[25] 18 U.S.C. § 3621(b).

BOP reported that it begins the process for community corrections placement approximately 17 to 24 months prior to an inmate's projected release date.

Based on the most recently available data, during fiscal year 2010, almost 29,000 inmates completed their sentences through community corrections. Of those inmates who were placed in community corrections, over 60 percent were placed in RRCs only while the remainder received a combination of RRC placement followed by home detention, or home detention only. For those inmates who did not receive placement in RRCs, BOP officials stated that these inmates, while eligible, may decline RRC placement or RRCs may not be able to accommodate them. For example, BOP officials stated that sex offenders are difficult to place since there are only a limited number of RRCs able to accept them. In fiscal year 2010, the average length of stay for inmates who were placed in community corrections ranged from approximately 147 days for those inmates who were placed in an RRC followed by home detention, to 95 days for inmates placed in an RRC not followed by home detention. Moreover, inmates who are eligible for home detention can be placed for up to 6 months or 10 percent of their sentences, whichever is less. In fiscal year 2010, of the 11,239 inmates who were placed in home detention either directly or following an RRC placement, 119 served either 6 months or 10 percent of their sentence in home detention. According to BOP officials at institutions we visited, decisions about length of stay in home detention are made on an individualized basis. It may take some inmates longer than others to have the necessary resources in place—such as a residence, a supportive family, and a job—to increase the likelihood of a successful home detention placement. In addition, inmates who have served longer sentences often have more serious needs upon release from prison that can best be met through participation in programs offered by RRCs rather than in home detention. Table 2 shows the number of eligible inmates placed in community corrections and the average length of stay during fiscal years 2009 and 2010.[26]

[26] According to BOP officials, data for fiscal year 2011 are not yet available because, as of December 2011, some inmates placed during fiscal year 2011 have not yet completed their sentences and been released from community corrections and BOP custody.

Table 2: Number of Eligible Inmates Placed in Community Corrections Who Complete Their Sentences, and Average Length of Stay for Fiscal Years 2009 and 2010

Type of placement	Fiscal Year 2009		Fiscal Year 2010	
	Number placed	Average length of stay (days)	Number placed	Average length of stay (days)
RRCs only	17,618	96	17,672	95
RRCs then home detention	10,452	150	11,094	147
Home detention only	143	83	145	103
Total placements in community corrections	**28,213**	**116**	**28,911**	**115**

Source: GAO analysis of BOP RRC and home detention utilization data.

According to BOP officials, strategic goals are set for RRC utilization at each security level BOP operates.[27] From fiscal years 2009 through 2011, BOP set goals of 65 percent utilization for high security, 70 percent for medium security, 75 percent for low security, and 85 percent for minimum security. According to BOP officials, high-security inmates may be more difficult to place than their counterparts at other security levels, due to the greater likelihood that inmates with high-security classifications are more likely to be violent offenders than inmates at other security levels. BOP documented that in fiscal years 2009 through 2011 it exceeded its goals in each security level.[28]

The average length of stay in an RRC for inmates at each security level also varied, with minimum-security inmates receiving longer stays than inmates at other security levels. Recognizing that inmates at higher risk for reoffending may be placed less often and may have shorter lengths of placements than inmates at lower risk of reoffending, a June 2010 memorandum from the BOP Correctional Programs Division states that higher risk inmates are more likely to benefit from RRC placement than lower risk inmates, in terms of their likelihood of reoffending.[29] Therefore, the memorandum recommends that RRC resources be focused on those higher risk inmates most likely to benefit from placements.

---

[27] Utilization refers to the percentage of eligible inmates BOP is able to place in RRCs.

[28] BOP Residential Re-Entry Utilization Reports.

[29] *Memorandum for Chief Executive Officers: Revised Guidance for Residential Reentry (RRC) Placements.* Assistant Director Scott Dodrill, BOP Correctional Programs Division, June 24, 2010.

GAO-12-320 BOP Use of Sentencing Flexibilities

BOP has also recently developed strategic goals for home detention. For fiscal year 2011, BOP had a goal to place 40 percent of all inmates eligible for community corrections in home detention. This goal includes direct designations to home detention as well as a combination of placement in an RRC followed by home detention. Moreover, in a June 2010 memorandum, BOP management encouraged institutions to consider opportunities to place minimum-security inmates in home detention. Specifically, the memo states that institution staff should evaluate minimum-security inmates to determine if direct transfer from an institution to home detention is appropriate. BOP officials told us that placing more minimum-security inmates in home detention would free up space in RRCs for higher risk inmates. Although BOP does not track home detention placements by security level, BOP data show that most of the inmates placed directly to home detention have a minimum-security designation.[30]

BOP reported that housing inmates in community corrections was more costly, on a per diem basis, than housing inmates in minimum- and low-security facilities. Based on the most recently available data, in fiscal year 2010 the daily cost of a community corrections bed on average was $70.79. Only the per diem costs for inmates in medium- and high-security facilities exceeded per diem costs for community corrections.[31] For example, BOP's per diem costs to house inmates in institutions of varying security levels were $57.55 for minimum, $69.53 for low, $71.91 for medium, and $92.76 for high security as reflected in figure 3.

---

[30] Although BOP does not routinely track home detention placement by security level, BOP was able to provide us with a snapshot of the data as of November 25, 2011. Of inmates on home detention, 1 percent were designated as high security, 14 percent as medium security, 22 percent as low security, and 63 percent as minimum security.

[31] We have ongoing work looking at facility and RRC costs in more detail, which we will report on later this year.

Figure 3: Daily Cost per Inmate of BOP Facilities Compared with Community Corrections

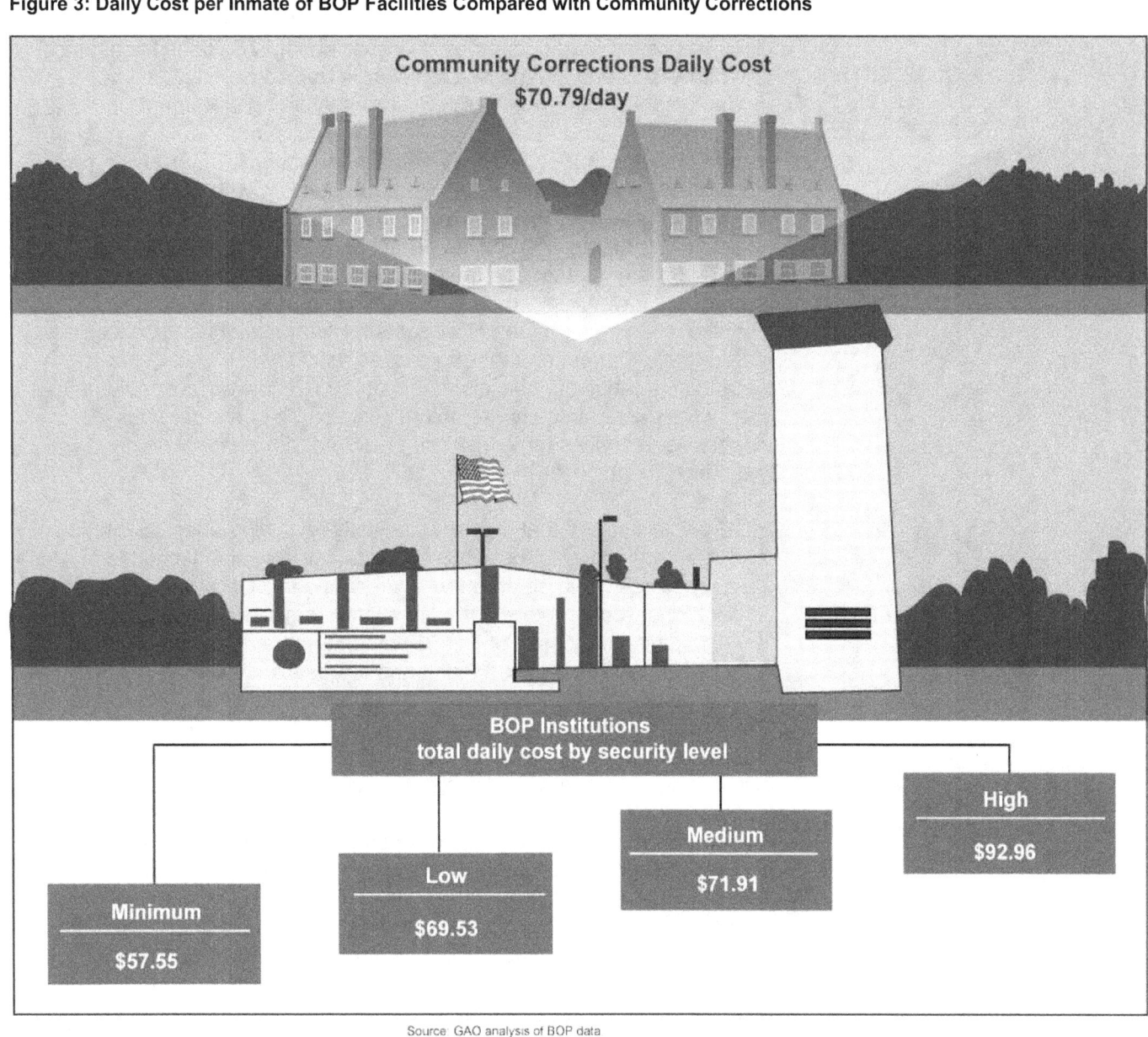

Source: GAO analysis of BOP data

For inmates in community corrections, the RRC is required to collect a subsistence fee of 25 percent of an inmate's gross income if that inmate is employed, to help defray the costs of community corrections placement. The subsistence payment is to be subtracted from the amount the RRC bills BOP for providing supervision of inmates. For example, one RRC we visited stated that they collected about $75,000 in fiscal year 2010 from working inmate residents. This translates to a little over $6,000 a month subtracted from the RRC's monthly billing statement.

In contracting with RRCs for community corrections, BOP pays a rate of 50 percent of the overall per diem rate negotiated with the RRC for each inmate in home detention. For example, if BOP pays a contractor the average community corrections per diem rate of $70.79, BOP would pay $35.39 per day for that contractor's supervision of each inmate in home detention. However, according to BOP, the agency does not require contractors to provide the actual costs for home detention services as part of their contract and therefore does not know the cost of home detention. In addition, officials at two of the RRCs we visited told us that they were uncertain as to the actual costs of the home detention supervision services they provided to BOP and had not explicitly examined these costs.

BOP officials stated that they are currently reviewing open solicitations and new requirements for RRC contracts, to determine locations in which cost proposals could be amended. According to BOP, the amended solicitations would require potential contractors to submit separate line items outlining the costs for RRC beds and home detention services separately. BOP has stated that it has a process underway to start to review contractors' proposals that would separate the price of home detention from the price of RRC beds, but BOP has not provided documentation of the review process or time frames and milestones for when it expects to finalize the process for requiring contractors to separate the price. In accordance with standard practices for program and project management, specific desired outcomes or results should be conceptualized and defined in the planning process as part of a road map, along with the appropriate projects needed to achieve those results, and milestones.[32] Without a plan for the development of this process, including time frames and milestones for when it will require contractors to submit separate prices for RRC beds and home detention services, BOP has no road map for how this will be achieved. Furthermore, setting time frames for developing its process could better position BOP to set a

---

[32] The Project Management Institute, *The Standard for Program Management* © (2006).

level of reimbursement to the RRCs that reflects the price of home detention, as well as weigh the costs and benefits of alternative options for supervising inmates in home detention.

Most Inmates Earn the Maximum Sentence Reduction for Good Conduct, and BOP Has Proposed Changes to the Amount

Most eligible inmates receive all of their potential GCT credit for compliance with institutional disciplinary regulations. An inmate who is serving a term of imprisonment of more than 1 year, other than a term of life imprisonment, may receive credit toward the service of his or her sentence, beyond the time served, known as GCT credit. Inmates who have earned, or are making satisfactory progress toward earning, a high school diploma or equivalent degree are eligible to receive 54 days of sentence credit at the end of each year served; otherwise, inmates are eligible to receive 42 days of sentence credit at the end of each year served. Sentence credit is prorated for the last partial year of a sentence served. From fiscal years 2009 through 2011, BOP data show that about 87 percent of inmates had earned all of their available GCT credit by the end of each year, and an additional 3 percent of inmates earned at least 90 percent of the maximum available GCT credit.[33]

Inmates may be disallowed from earning a certain number of days of GCT credit for committing disciplinary infractions of a certain severity level. An institution's Disciplinary Hearing Officer (DHO) is the sole official with the authority to disallow an inmate's GCT credit. If the DHO finds an inmate guilty of an infraction following a disciplinary hearing, the amount of GCT credit he or she disallows is to be based on the severity of the infraction and the number of times an inmate has committed an offense of the same level of severity.[34] For example, an inmate has to commit a low-severity infraction three times within the same year for disallowance of GCT credit to occur. However, an inmate who commits a greatest severity infraction once is subject to GCT disallowance. Table 3 shows the GCT credit disallowance guidelines by infraction severity level.

---

[33] BOP tracks inmates' earned GCT credit throughout their terms of imprisonment.

[34] DHO hearings are held for infractions at the 100-level (greatest severity) and 200-level (high severity) as well as for repeated lower severity infractions or any cases referred by institution staff. Inmates may appeal the DHO's decision through BOP's administrative remedy process, which may include reviews at the regional and headquarters levels.

Table 3: GCT Credit Disallowance Guidelines, by Infraction Severity Level

Infraction severity level	Infraction examples	Repetition during year	Minimum disallowance[a]
100-Level (Greatest severity)	Assaults; escapes; riots; drug or alcohol use	1	41 days or 75% of remaining GCT
200-Level (High severity)	Fights; bribes; theft; tattooing	1	27 days or 50% of remaining GCT
300-Level (Moderate severity)	Insolence; gambling; lying; gang activities	2	14 days or 25% of remaining GCT
400-Level (Low severity)	Obscene language; disruptive conduct	3	7 days or 12.5% of remaining GCT

Source: BOP Program Statement 5270 09: Inmate Discipline Program.

[a] If an inmate has less than 54 days of GCT credit remaining during a given year, the minimum disallowance for an infraction is set at a percentage of the inmate's remaining GCT credit.

For certain infractions, GCT credit that was earned in prior years may also be forfeited.[35] GCT credit that has been disallowed or forfeited may not later be restored. The DHO has discretion to depart from the GCT credit disallowance guidelines or to forfeit an inmate's earned GCT credit based on mitigating or aggravating circumstances. If an inmate is a first-time offender and is involved in BOP programs, demonstrating a commitment to rehabilitation, a DHO may elect to reduce the amount of or refrain from a GCT credit disallowance. Alternatively, if an inmate is a repeat offender or commits an egregious act, the DHO may increase the GCT credit disallowance or forfeit the inmate's earned GCT credit. Whenever the DHO departs from the disallowance guidelines, he or she is required to provide justification for the departure and an explanation of the mitigating or aggravating circumstances in the DHO hearing report filed with the regional management office.[36] For example, in fiscal year 2011, BOP DHOs departed from the disallowance guidelines 17,571 times, or in 37 percent of DHO hearings, most often disallowing less GCT credit than called for in the corresponding guideline.[37] The six DHOs we spoke with in BOP's Western and Mid-Atlantic regions described the discipline process in consistent terms and five of the six DHOs recounted the same types of mitigating and aggravating circumstances they

---

[35] Earned GCT credit does not vest until an inmate's release date, meaning that all credit is vulnerable to forfeiture for disciplinary cause.

[36] The decision of the DHO is final and subject to review by the Regional Director to ensure conformity with the discipline policy.

[37] In fiscal year 2011, of the 17,571 times DHOs departed from the guidelines, 14,227 were downward departures and 3,344 were upward departures.

GAO-12-320 BOP Use of Sentencing Flexibilities

generally considered for departures.[38] For example, DHOs cited first-time offenses and being taken advantage of as common mitigating circumstances. One DHO we spoke with reduced a newer inmate's disallowance because the inmate was manipulated by a fellow inmate to make a prohibited phone call for him. DHOs cited repeated offenses, egregious acts, and violence against correctional officers as common aggravating circumstances. One DHO we spoke with recalled forfeiting over 300 days of an inmate's earned GCT credit after the inmate was involved in a prison riot. The six DHOs we spoke with told us that the disallowance guidelines were clear, and that the discretion to depart from the guidelines offered them sufficient flexibility and latitude to successfully impact inmate behavior.

Although most prisoners receive all of their potential GCT credit, BOP's method of awarding GCT credit at the end of each year an inmate serves results in a maximum of 47 days of GCT credit earned per year of sentence imposed rather than the 54 days that inmates who have contested BOP's method in court maintain was the original intent of the statute.[39] Under the Sentencing Reform Act, the USSC established sentence guidelines with the understanding that inmates would receive GCT credit so that their actual time served would be 85 percent of the length of the sentence imposed by the judge, assuming good behavior.[40] BOP's method of awarding GCT, however, results in inmates serving more than 85 percent of their imposed sentences, even after earning the maximum GCT credit, as can be seen in table 4, for a hypothetical sentence of 10 years imposed by the sentencing judge.

---

[38] One of the six DHOs did not recall departing from the guidelines in recent years.

[39] As authorized in statute, 18 U.S.C. § 3624(b), BOP awards "up to 54 days at the end of each year of the prisoner's term of imprisonment," or 54 days per year of sentence served. As applied by BOP, this results in 47 days earned per year of sentence imposed because inmates do not earn GCT credit for years they do not ultimately serve due to being released early.

[40] United States Sentencing Commission, *Supplementary Report on the Initial Sentencing Guidelines and Policy Statements*, 23 (1987).

Table 4: Illustration of BOP's Calculation of GCT Credit for an Imposed Sentence of 10 years for an Inmate Earning the Maximum GCT Credit

Sentence completed	GCT granted at end of year	Time remaining on sentence, in years and days
0 years	Not applicable	10 years (3,650 days)
1 year	54	8 years, 311 days
2 years	54	7 years, 257 days
3 years	54	6 years, 203 days
4 years	54	5 years, 149 days
5 years	54	4 years, 95 days
6 years	54	3 years, 41 days
7 years	54	1 year, 352 days
8 years	54	298 days
Inmate released during 9th year, after completing 8 years and 260 days	38 (GCT for the remaining 298 days is prorated to conform to the ratio of 54 days per 365 served)	
Total GCT days granted	470	
Total GCT days granted per year of sentence imposed	470/10=47	
Total time served (days)	3,650-470=3,180	
Percent of sentence served	3,180/3,650 = 87.1 %	

Source: GAO analysis of BOP GCT credit calculation.

The U.S. Supreme Court upheld BOP's methodology against a challenge brought by inmate petitioners.[41] However, BOP officials told us that the agency was supportive of amending the statute, and had submitted a legislative proposal to Congress such that 54 days would be provided for each year of the term of imprisonment originally imposed by the judge, which would result in inmates serving 85 percent of their sentence.[42] BOP

---

[41] *Barber v. Thomas*, 130 S. Ct. 2499 (2010).

[42] The additional credit would be awarded retroactively to inmates sentenced under the Sentencing Reform Act prior to the legislative change. For the hypothetical inmate with a 10-year sentence described in table 4, the inmate would receive a total of 540 days of GCT. Thus the inmate would serve 3,110 days (85 percent) of the 3,650 days sentence imposed by the judge.

provided us estimates in December 2011 showing that if the GCT credit allowance was increased by 7 days, as proposed, BOP could save over $40 million in the first fiscal year after the policy change from the early release of about 3,900 inmates. As of December 2011, the legislative proposal had not been introduced on the floors of the House or Senate.[43]

BOP Has Used Other Authorities Less Frequently to Reduce Federal Prisoners' Periods of Incarceration

Modification of an imposed sentence: BOP has authority to motion the court to reduce an inmate's sentence in certain statutorily authorized circumstances, but that authority is implemented infrequently, if at all.

- The court, upon motion of the Director of BOP, may reduce the term of imprisonment after considering certain statutory factors to the extent that they are applicable,[44] if it finds that "extraordinary and compelling reasons warrant such a reduction" (also known as "compassionate release") and the reduction is consistent with applicable policy statements issued by the USSC.[45] According to BOP officials, the Director has motioned sentencing judges for inmates' early releases in a limited number of cases. For instance, BOP has historically interpreted "extraordinary and compelling circumstances" as limited to cases where the inmate has a terminal illness with a life expectancy of 1 year or less or has a profoundly debilitating medical condition. The USSC issued guidance that listed a number of additional circumstances, such as the death or incapacitation of the inmate's only family member capable of caring for the inmate's minor child or children.[46] As of December 2011, BOP had not revised its written policy to explicitly include all of the circumstances noted in the USSC guidance although, according to BOP officials, the agency is reviewing two cases that would fall within these circumstances. Where "extraordinary and compelling circumstances" may exist, inmates

---

[43] Second Chance Reauthorization Act of 2011, S.1231, 112th Cong. § 4(f) proposes to amend certain statutory provisions related to good conduct time in 18 U.S.C. § 3624(b)(1). The bill was reported out of the Senate Judiciary Committee on July 21, 2011, and is awaiting full Senate action. Similar legislation has not yet been introduced in the House.

[44] 18 U.S.C. § 3553(a).

[45] 18 U.S.C. § 3582(c)(1)(A)(i).

[46] Under 28 U.S.C. § 994(t), the USSC, in promulgating general policy statements regarding the sentencing modification provisions in 18 U.S.C. § 3582(c)(1)(A), is required to describe what should be considered extraordinary and compelling reasons for sentence reduction, including the criteria to be applied and a list of specific examples.

generally must submit a request explaining their circumstances and their plans for housing, financial support, and medical care if granted an early release. The request is to proceed through multiple layers of review, including the inmate's warden, the Regional Director, BOP's Office of General Counsel, and the BOP Director, who may ultimately motion the court.[47] BOP officials recorded that from calendar years 2009 through 2011, 55 requests for early release were approved by the BOP Director and brought as motions to a sentencing judge out of 89 requests approved at lower levels and received at BOP headquarters.[48]

- The court, upon motion of the Director of BOP, may reduce a prison term after considering certain statutory factors to the extent that they are applicable, if (1) an inmate is over 70 years old, (2) has served at least 30 years in prison pursuant to certain sentences imposed by statute,[49] (3) a determination has been made by the BOP Director that the inmate is not a danger to the safety of any other person or the community as provided by statute,[50] and (4) such a reduction is consistent with applicable policy statements issued by the USSC.[51] However, according to BOP officials, since the authority was enacted, BOP has had no inmates in its custody meeting these criteria and is considering how to implement this authority in the future if an inmate qualified.

- Generally, where a term of imprisonment is based upon a sentencing range that has subsequently been lowered by the USSC, upon motion of the BOP Director, the court may reduce the term of imprisonment.[52] According to BOP officials the BOP Director does not directly motion the sentencing judge because this is generally accomplished by the U.S. Attorney's Office as the litigating body of DOJ. In addition, BOP officials also stated that it is not necessary for the BOP Director to

---

[47] A denial at the warden or Regional Director level may be appealed within BOP through an administrative relief process. A denial by BOP's Office of General Counsel or Director is considered a final agency decision and can be appealed by motion to the federal court.

[48] Additionally, as of December 2011, five requests submitted in fiscal year 2011 were still under review at BOP headquarters.

[49] 18 U.S.C. § 3559(c).

[50] 18 U.S.C. § 3142(g).

[51] 18 U.S.C. § 3582(c)(1)(A)(ii).

[52] 18 U.S.C. § 3582(c)(2). The court may also act upon the motion of the defendant or its own motion to reduce the term of imprisonment.

GAO-12-320 BOP Use of Sentencing Flexibilities

motion the judge because inmates and their counsel generally initiate the process. BOP supports the process in other ways, including educating inmates about the relevant guidelines changes, notifying the U.S. Attorneys Offices if inmates who appear to be eligible are missed, and processing inmate sentence reductions if granted by a sentencing judge. BOP has estimated that the retroactive change to the sentencing guidelines for crack cocaine offenses that went into effect on November 1, 2011, will result in 2,391 additional inmates being released from BOP custody from fiscal years 2012 through 2014, yielding an estimated cost savings of $160 million.[53]

Early release prior to a weekend or holiday: BOP releases inmates on the last preceding weekday prior to a release date that falls on a Saturday, Sunday, or legal holiday.

Shock Incarceration Program: Although BOP retains the authority to operate the shock incarceration program, also known as boot camps, it discontinued the program in 2005 due to its cost and research showing that it was not effective in reducing inmate recidivism. Nonviolent, volunteer, minimum-security inmates serving sentences of more than 12 months but not more than 30 months were eligible for the program, which combined features of military basic training with traditional BOP correctional values to promote personal development, self-control, and discipline.[54] Throughout the typical 6-month program, inmate participants were required to adhere to a highly regimented schedule of strict discipline, physical training, hard labor, drill, job training, educational programs, and substance abuse counseling. BOP provided inmates who successfully completed the program and were serving sentences of 12 to 30 months with a sentence reduction of up to 6 months. All inmates who successfully completed the program were eligible to serve the remainder of their sentences in community corrections locations, such as RRCs or

---

[53] A similar retroactive change to the sentencing guidelines for crack cocaine went into effect on November 1, 2007. As of June 2011, the USSC reported that of the 25,736 inmate applicants for a sentence reduction, 16,511 (64.2 percent) had been granted. Eligible inmates received an average sentence reduction of 26 months. The USSC was able to determine the origin of the motion for 15,016 of the inmates who were granted a sentence reduction. The BOP Director brought the motion in none of those cases. *U.S. Sentencing Commission Preliminary Crack Cocaine Retroactivity Data Report, June 2011.*

[54] Inmates serving sentences of 30 to 60 months and within 24 months of their projected release dates were also eligible to participate in the program, but were not eligible for the sentence reduction upon completion.

home detention. A study of one of BOP's shock incarceration programs, published in September 1996, found that the program had no effect on participants' recidivism rates.[55] According to BOP officials, those and other evaluation findings and the cost of the program led BOP to discontinue its use in 2005.

Elderly Offender Pilot Program: Authorization for BOP's elderly offender home detention pilot program expired in September 2010. Generally, the 2-year pilot program enabled BOP to transfer to home detention inmates who were at least 65 years old, had served at least 10 years and 75 percent of their non-life sentences, had no history of violence, sexual offenses, or escape or attempted escape from a BOP institution, and who BOP determined would be of no substantial risk of engaging in criminal conduct or endangering any person or the public if released and with respect to whom BOP had determined that release to home detention will result in a substantial net reduction of costs to the federal government.[56] During the program, 71 inmates were transferred to home detention. The statute requires the Attorney General to monitor and evaluate each eligible elderly offender placed on home detention, and report to Congress concerning the experience with the program. According to BOP officials, this report has not been completed. We have ongoing work looking at the results and costs of the pilot in more detail, which we will report on later this year.

Concurrent versus consecutive sentences: When both a federal and a state court have imposed prison sentences on an offender, BOP has the authority to credit time served in a state institution towards an inmate's federal sentence in certain circumstances, thus resulting in a concurrent sentence, but this authority applies to a relatively limited number of inmates.[57] According to BOP's program statement, multiple terms of imprisonment imposed at different times run consecutively unless the

---

[55] Federal Bureau of Prisons, *An Evaluation of the Federal Bureau of Prisons Lewisburg Intensive Confinement Center* (September 1996).

[56] 42 U.S.C. § 17541(g)(5)(A).

[57] With a concurrent sentence, two or more sentences of imprisonment are to be served simultaneously. For example, generally, if a defendant receives concurrent sentences of 10 years and 15 years, the total amount of time for imprisonment is 15 years.

federal sentencing judge orders that they run concurrently.[58] This includes cases when a federal judge has not stated whether a state and federal sentence should run concurrently or consecutively. However, BOP may review, or the inmates may petition BOP to review, their cases to determine a federal sentencing judge's intent. BOP reviews the inmate's sentencing documents and custody history, and may also contact the federal sentencing judge to determine whether the judge intended that the state and federal sentences should be served consecutively or concurrently. For example, of the 538 cases BOP reviewed in fiscal year 2011, 99 requests to serve sentences concurrently were granted, for a total of about 118,700 days of sentence credit, 386 were not granted, and 53 were still under review as of the end of fiscal year 2011.[59]

Credit for criminal custody: BOP has the authority to grant credit for time served in criminal custody (such as time spent awaiting trial), and according to BOP policy, it considers detention by Immigration and Customs Enforcement (ICE) for the purposes of deportation to be administrative custody until criminal charges are brought against a detainee. According to BOP officials, BOP reviews inmate records for any criminal custody time that could be credited towards an inmate's federal sentence. BOP reviewers may contact ICE for clarification of an inmate's custody record, but, according to BOP officials, the various ICE districts keep records differently and a clear determination of when a federal charge was filed and an inmate's criminal custody began may be difficult to achieve.

---

[58] With consecutive sentences, two or more sentences of imprisonment are to be served in sequence. For example, generally, if a defendant receives consecutive sentences of 10 years and 12 years, the total amount of time for imprisonment is 22 years.

[59] Although BOP considers the federal judge's recommendation, if obtained, BOP officials stated that each case is evaluated on an individual basis, using factors such as the history and characteristics of the prisoner, the resources of state facilities where the inmate will be serving the federal sentence concurrent with the state sentence, the inmate's disciplinary record while at the state institution, and whether the federal statute under which an inmate is convicted precludes the sentences from being served concurrently, for example, conviction for aggravated identity theft combined with a conviction for any other offense.

Inmate Eligibility and Lack of Capacity Impact BOP's Use of Certain Flexibilities

Certain Inmates' Ineligibility for Community Corrections Impacts BOP's Use of RRCs and RDAP

BOP officials cited inmate ineligibility for placement in community corrections as the number one reason that all inmates do not get released through RRCs and one of the chief reasons that some inmates are precluded from participating in RDAP.[60] Specifically, BOP's RRC program statement prohibits certain inmates from placement in an RRC. For example, inmates with detainers, with sentences of 6 months or less, who refuse to satisfy BOP's Financial Responsibility Program, or who are in civil commitment status are all ineligible for RRC placement.[61] According to BOP, inmates with detainers are deemed inappropriate for placement in community corrections due to the increased risk of escape and for those with immigration detainers, the likelihood of deportation. Moreover, all inmates who have financial obligations, whether court-ordered restitution, court fees, or tax liabilities, must comply with the Financial Responsibility Program to participate in programming including community corrections.[62] This ineligibility for RRC placement also disqualifies an inmate from placement in home detention. Figure 4 shows the number of inmates ineligible for RRC placement from April 2008 to March 2011.

---

[60] To participate in the RDAP program, inmates must be able to complete all components of the program, including the RRC portion.

[61] A detainer is a document issued by a law enforcement entity, a jail, or correctional facility to seek custody of an individual for purposes of instituting legal proceedings. The Financial Responsibility Program assists inmates in meeting any financial obligations imposed by the sentencing court. An inmate who has a commitment status is held as a material witness; held due to an administrative commitment (holdover and pretrial inmates); or held by BOP for ICE.

[62] The Victim and Witness Protection Act of 1982, Pub. L. No. 97-291, 96 Stat. 1248, the Victims of Crime Act of 1984, Pub. L. No. 98-473, 98 Stat. 2170, the Comprehensive Crime Control Act of 1984, Pub. L. No. 98-473, 98 Stat. 1976 and the Federal Debt Collection Procedures Act of 1990, Pub. L. No. 101-647, 104 Stat. 4933, require a diligent effort on the part of all law enforcement agencies to collect court-ordered financial obligations.

Figure 4: Number of Inmates Ineligible for RRC placement from April 2008 to March 2011

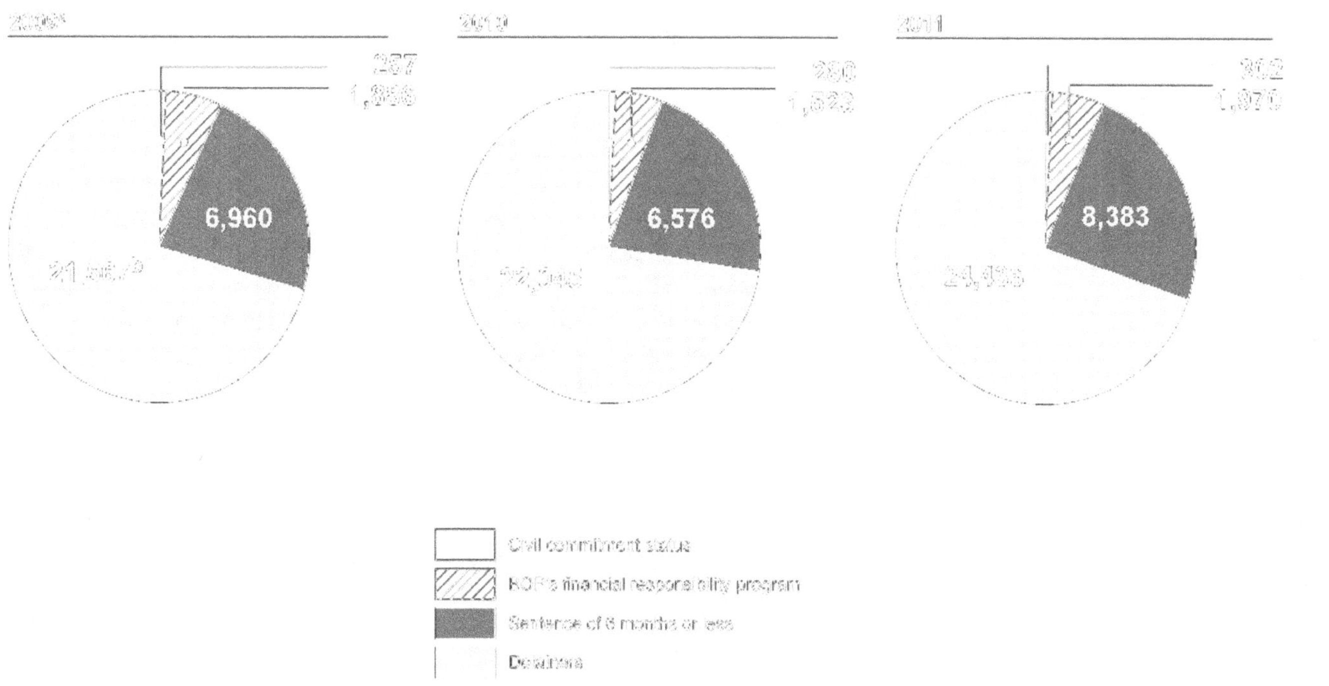

Source: GAO analysis of BOP RRC utilization data.

[a] Data provided by BOP for the following periods: 2009: April 1, 2008, to March 31, 2009; 2010: April 1, 2009, to March 31, 2010; 2011: April 1, 2010, to March 31, 2011.

[b] Some inmates are counted in more than one category.

BOP officials stated that certain offenses committed by inmates may also make it difficult for BOP to place them in RRCs. For example, according to BOP officials, some RRCs are required to enter into agreements with communities regarding the type of inmates they will house and some communities have enacted local laws that prohibit the placement of certain inmates such as sex offenders and arsonists in a communal setting. Other reasons inmates may not be placed in RRCs include the inmate's refusal to be placed or the inmate's medical or mental health needs that could not be accommodated at the RRC. According to BOP officials, inmates may refuse RRC placement for a variety of reasons but the reasons for refusal cited most often by officials during our site visits to BOP facilities included:

- some RRC accommodations are perceived by some inmates to be subpar compared to prisons;
- some minimum-security and low-security inmates do not want to reside in RRCs with higher security inmates; and
- some inmates do not want to pay the 25 percent subsistence fee.

To participate in RDAP, inmates must be able to complete both the institution and the RRC components of the program. As a result, inmates who are prohibited from transferring to RRCs are excluded from RDAP. For instance, BOP estimates that 2,500 criminal aliens would participate in RDAP each year, but are ineligible due to immigration detainers. Prior to a 1996 BOP policy change, inmates with detainers could complete the program by participating in transitional treatment within a BOP institution. However, according to BOP officials, transitional treatment within an institution is ineffective because the inmate remains sheltered from the partial freedoms and outside pressures experienced during an RRC placement.

Realizing that potential cost savings could result from early releases of criminal aliens, among other reasons, BOP is considering changing its policy and allowing eligible nonviolent criminal aliens to complete the RDAP program without the RRC component and receive sentence reductions of up to 1 year for successful completion.[63] According to BOP, this policy shift would require a rule change and the development of procedures to ensure that no U.S. citizen was displaced from participating in RDAP. BOP officials stated that decisions on this issue would not be made until expanded program capacity becomes available, which is currently uncertain.

Lack of Available Capacity Impacts BOP's Use of RRCs and RDAP

A lack of RRC beds limits BOP's ability to further utilize RRC placements. Based on the most recently available data, in fiscal year 2010, about 29,000 inmates spent time in an RRC prior to release from BOP custody. Although BOP officials at institutions we visited stated that they assessed inmates on a case-by-case basis to determine the appropriate RRC placement length, the officials stated that referrals can be reduced due to RRC capacity constraints. According to BOP officials, in fiscal year 2010, about 2.7 percent of eligible inmates were denied placement due to a lack of bed space. BOP faces challenges in increasing its RRC bed space

---

[63] BOP provided us estimates of savings of $25 million per year.

capacity, which limits its ability to increase the length of RRC placements. According to BOP community corrections officials, BOP has difficulty acquiring new RRC contracts and increasing its RRC capacity because of local zoning restrictions and the unwillingness of many communities to accept nearby RRCs.

Although the Second Chance Act increased BOP's flexibility to place inmates in RRCs for up to 12 months, as reported by BOP officials, challenges facing the expansion of its RRC capacity limit the impact of this increased flexibility.[64] As of November 2011, BOP reported that available contracted RRC bed space was 8,859 estimated beds. For each available RRC bed, BOP can transfer one inmate to the RRC for a maximum of 12 months, or BOP could send multiple inmates for shorter placements (e.g., three inmates for 4 months each). As such, for this increased flexibility to have an impact on the average length of RRC placements, RRC capacity would need to increase. To provide all eligible inmates with the maximum allowable 12 months in an RRC, BOP would require about 29,000 available beds annually.

Some inmates are more affected by capacity constraints than others, such as those with criminal records of sex offenses or those being released into urban areas with few RRCs. According to BOP, only a limited number of RRCs are able to accept sex offenders, and thus BOP, at the onset, has a limited number of RRC beds for sex offender placement. In addition, inmates releasing to urban areas may have their placement lengths reduced due to capacity constraints. For example, BOP staff we interviewed during our site visits identified shortages of RRC beds in Southern California, North Carolina, and the Washington, D.C. metropolitan area affecting the length of RRC placements. When referring inmates for RRC placements, BOP considers the inmate's original sentencing location to facilitate transition and successful reentry. As such, BOP's utilization of RRC placements is limited in geographical areas that do not have enough RRC beds to accommodate returning inmates.

According to BOP officials, systemwide program capacity similarly constrains BOP's utilization of RDAP sentence reductions—specifically, BOP's ability to admit RDAP participants early enough to earn their

---

[64] Pub. L. No. 110-199, 122 Stat. 657, 692-93.

maximum allowable sentence reductions. BOP officials stated that the RDAP sentence reduction incentive caused a backlog for entry into the program. Long wait lists resulted in inmates entering RDAP with insufficient time to complete the program in time to receive the maximum sentence reduction. In fiscal years 2007 and 2008, BOP reported to Congress that long wait lists (over 7,600 systemwide) prevented some eligible inmates from participating in the program at all—20 percent and 7 percent unable to participate, respectively. RDAP capacity, as measured by the number of program slots open to inmates at one time throughout BOP (6,685 in fiscal year 2011), has grown at a relatively steady rate since the program began in fiscal year 1989, and increased by 400 slots from fiscal years 2009 to 2011. According to BOP officials, as program capacity has increased in recent years, wait lists have been reduced, even with continued growth in the inmate population. This has enabled inmates to enter the program sooner and resulted in an increase in the percentage of eligible inmates who complete RDAP and receive the maximum sentence reductions from 14 percent in fiscal year 2009 to 25 percent in fiscal year 2011. However, according to BOP officials, RDAP is still catching up to the increased demand and continues to have wait lists.

According to BOP officials, wait lists for entry into RDAP are currently prioritized in accordance with statute based on inmates' proximity to their projected release dates which include GCT credit expected to be earned, but do not include the potential RDAP sentence reduction that eligible participants may earn. Two subject matter experts who advocate for inmate interests whom we spoke with stated that BOP could consider including the potential RDAP sentence reduction in inmates' projected release date calculations. This could ensure that eligible inmates would enter the program sooner and in enough time to receive the maximum reduction. For example, if two inmates have the same projected release date, after accounting for GCT credit, but one inmate would be eligible for a 1-year sentence reduction on completion of RDAP while the other would not be eligible for a sentence reduction upon completion of RDAP, the inmate eligible for the sentence reduction would have a higher position on the wait list for entry into RDAP than the inmate ineligible for a sentence reduction. BOP has stated that if it were to prioritize RDAP entry in this way, some inmates who are not eligible for the sentence reduction would not be able to enter the program at all, as they would continually be displaced on the wait lists by inmates who are eligible for the sentence reduction. BOP is required by statute, subject to the availability of appropriations, to provide residential substance abuse treatment for all eligible inmates, regardless of their eligibility for the sentence reduction incentive, and thus must ensure that all eligible inmates are able to participate in the program prior to their release from custody. However, BOP was unable to provide documentation that including RDAP sentence reduction in computation of the projected release date would continually displace inmates eligible for RDAP but ineligible for the associated sentence reduction.

BOP's fiscal year 2012 budget request included an increase of $15 million for RDAP, which was not funded. According to BOP, the funding would have reduced RDAP wait lists and enabled eligible inmates to enter the program early enough to earn their maximum allowable sentence reductions. BOP stated that the $15 million increase would have covered 125 new drug treatment staff positions and would have allowed an additional 4,000 inmates to complete RDAP annually.[65] BOP officials also told us that if BOP changes its policy to allow criminal aliens to participate in RDAP, the funding increase for RDAP proposed in the 2012 budget request would have been sufficient to allow this additional inmate population to participate in RDAP without impacting the ability of U.S. citizens to participate and receive the maximum available sentence reductions.

Timely program admission would result in future cost savings through additional sentence reductions. For example, if every eligible RDAP participant who completed the program in fiscal year 2011 had received their maximum sentence reduction, BOP would have been responsible for 15,729 fewer months of inmate incarceration, yielding an estimated cost savings of about $13.2 million. BOP estimated that allowing criminal aliens to participate in RDAP and earn sentence reductions could offer about $25 million of additional cost savings each year.

Conclusions

Federal inmate populations have been increasing and BOP is operating at more than a third over capacity. In addition, the absence of parole in the federal system and other federal statutes limit BOP's authority to modify an inmate's period of incarceration. Inmates, who earn their good conduct time, as most do, end up serving about 87 percent of their sentences. BOP's housing of inmates in community-based facilities or home detention is a key flexibility it uses to affect a prisoner's period of

---

[65] BOP has stated that it is unable to isolate the cost of RDAP programs from all BOP substance abuse treatment programs because staff who provide RDAP treatment also provide nonresidential and other drug treatment and education programs.

incarceration. However, BOP does not require its RRC contractors to separate the price of home detention services from the price of RRC beds. As a result, BOP lacks information on the price of home detention that could assist it in weighing the costs and benefits of alternative options for supervising inmates in home detention. While BOP is working to develop a process to require contractors to submit separate prices for the price of RRC beds and home detention services, without establishing a plan, including a time frame for development, BOP does not have a road map for how it will achieve this goal.

Recommendation for Executive Action

To determine the cost of home detention and potentially achieve cost savings, we recommend that the Director of BOP establish a plan, including time frames and milestones for completion, for requiring contractors to submit separate prices of RRC beds and home detention services.

Agency Comments and Our Evaluation

We provided a draft of this report to DOJ for its review and comment. BOP provided written comments on the draft report, which are reproduced in full in appendix I. BOP concurred with the findings in the report. Prior to receiving BOP's comment letter, on January 20, 2012, BOP's audit liaison requested that the wording of our recommendation be changed from "requiring contractors to identify RRC costs and home detention costs separately" to "requiring contractors to submit separate prices of RRC beds and home detention services." He stated that BOP was requesting this change because contractors are not required to disclose financial information, such as the actual costs to them of providing services to inmates, to BOP. Furthermore, the liaison stated that obtaining separate prices of RRC and home detention services will enable BOP to determine the price reasonableness of these services. We believe that BOP's proposed language addressed the intent of our recommendation, and thus we modified the recommendation language. BOP concurred with our recommendation, as revised, and also provided technical comments which we incorporated into the report, as appropriate.

We are sending copies of this report to the Attorney General, selected congressional committees, and other interested parties. In addition, this report will also be available at no charge on the GAO website at http://www.gao.gov.

If you or your staff have any further questions about this report, please contact me at (202) 512-9627 or maurerd@gao.gov. Contact points for our Offices of Congressional Relations and Public Affairs may be found on the last page of this report. Key contributors to this report are listed in appendix II.

David C. Maurer
Director, Homeland Security and Justice Issues

Appendix I: Comments from the Federal Bureau of Prisons

U.S. Department of Justice

Federal Bureau of Prisons

Office of the Director   _Washington, DC 20534_

January 25, 2012

David C. Maurer, Director
Homeland Security and Justice Issues
Government Accountability Office
Washington, DC 20548

Dear Mr. Maurer:

The Bureau of Prisons (BOP) appreciates the opportunity to formally respond to the Government Accountability Office's draft report entitled Eligibility and Capacity Impact Use of Flexibilities to Reduce Inmates' Time in Prison.

We have completed our review of the draft report. Our response to the Recommendation for Executive Action is as follows:

Recommendation: To determine the cost of home detention and potentially achieve cost savings, we recommend that the Director of BOP establish a plan, including a time frame and milestones for completion, for requiring contractors to submit separate line items for the price of RRC beds and home detention services.

Response: The BOP concurs with the recommendation.

If you have any questions regarding this response, please contact H. J. Marberry, Assistant Director, Program Review Division, at (202)353-2302.

Sincerely,

Charles E. Samuels, Jr.
Director

Appendix II: GAO Contact and Staff Acknowledgments

GAO Contact	David C. Maurer, (202) 512-9627 or maurerd@gao.gov.
Staff Acknowledgments	In addition to the contact named above, Chris Currie, Assistant Director; Tom Jessor; Bintou Njie; Michael Kniss; Billy Commons, III; Pedro Almoguera; and Lara Miklozek made significant contributions to this report.